8119

SO-BBP-604

Purchase 15.95 Smart Apple 2000

Published by Creative Education
123 South Broad Street, Mankato, Minnesota 56001
Creative Education is an imprint of The Creative Company

Designed by Stephanie Blumenthal
Production design by The Design Lab

Photographs by AP/Wide World Photo, Archive Photos, Columbia Pictures,
Corbis-Bettmann, D.M.I. Photos, Everett Collection, Fotos International,
Richard Hoffman, Premier, Reuters, and Universal Studios

Library of Congress Cataloging-in-Publication Data

Gish, Melissa
Steven Spielberg / by Melissa Gish
p. cm. – (Ovations)
Summary: A biography of the filmmaker whose creative drive has
led him to make many different kinds of movies, including *Jaws,
E.T., Schindler's List,* and *Saving Private Ryan.*
ISBN 0-88682-832-5

1. Spielberg, Steven, 1947– –Juvenile literature. 2. Motion Picture
producers and directors–United States–Biography–Juvenile literature.
[1. Spielberg, Steven, 1947-. 2. Motion picture producers and directors.]
I. Title. II. Series: Ovations (Mankato, Minn.)
PN1998.3.S65G57   1999
791.43'.0233'092–dc21
[B]   98-46787

First edition

2   4   6   8   9   7   5   3   1

STEVEN

SPIELBERG

BY MELISSA GISH

Creative C Education

REFLECTIONS

Agray mist hangs in the cold, early dawn air as ocean swells break on the shore of Omaha Beach. It is June 6, 1944. The first wave of the invasion known as D-Day is about to take place. Hundreds of men from the 1st U.S. Infantry Division stand poised on the decks of dozens of Higgins boats, awaiting the command to charge the beach.

Now fast-forward more than 50 years to another cold, early dawn, where another group of men who resemble those soldiers from 1944 are placed on a beach that resembles Omaha; and they wait not for a command from their general, but from the man directing them on film.

Suddenly a voice booms over a loudspeaker. "Action!" Mayhem erupts:

gunfire, smoke, explosions, men charging the beach, falling, crying out, dying, and the lapping waves turning red with blood. As a dozen cameramen capture scenes of violence, terror, and agony from all sides, one person struggles through the maze with his own small handheld camera in search of the most important thing he can put to film: reality. He is Steven Spielberg, and this carefully orchestrated chaos is the first 27 minutes of his World War II epic, *Saving Private Ryan.*

"I wanted to achieve reality," Spielberg said of *Private Ryan*, the movie that respected film critic Gene Siskel once called "a superb achievement by Steven Spielberg—again." In *Private Ryan*, the director's commitment to accuracy is evident. "I would be doing an extreme disservice to veterans if this was simply one more movie that glamorized World War II."

A sense of reality—and a sense of wonder—are the two most crucial elements in every Spielberg film, from the out-of-this-world characters in

E.T.: The Extra-Terrestrial and *Close Encounters of the Third Kind* to the terrifying beasts in *Jaws* and *Jurassic Park*. As writer Tim Appelo observes, Spielberg "has put more perception-changing images, more *pictures* into the minds of more people than any director who has ever lived." In short, Spielberg creates films that touch our hearts and spark our imaginations in ways that few films can.

From a young age Steven Spielberg has made movies the essence of his life. He made short films as a teenager, sneaked onto studio lots to watch professionals in action, and though he never attended film school, he learned the art and craft of movie-making by immersing himself in every aspect of production—from directing to filming to editing.

"He ate, breathed, and slept film," said producer Denis Hoffman. "His dream was to be a director, plain and simple. . . . It's not an accident Spielberg is where he is, it's not luck, it's all a plan he had."

On the movie set, Steven's creative mind works fast, yet he values feedback from his cast, film crew, and colleagues such as George Lucas, bottom.

EVOLUTION

On December 18, 1946, Steven Allan Spielberg was born at the Jewish Hospital in Cincinnati, Ohio. His father, Arnold, had been a radio operator during World War II and was now a computer engineer, designing and programming some of the earliest computers. Steven would later credit his father with fostering in him a fascination with computers and technology, as well as a respect for veterans of World War II and the stories they carried with them. The creative, artistic side of Steven's personality was drawn from his mother, Leah, who studied classical piano as a young woman and who later, as a mother of four, fostered her children's interest in the arts.

Steven's siblings were all girls. Anne was born on Christmas Day 1949, Susan was born in 1953, and Nancy in 1956. Many vital elements of

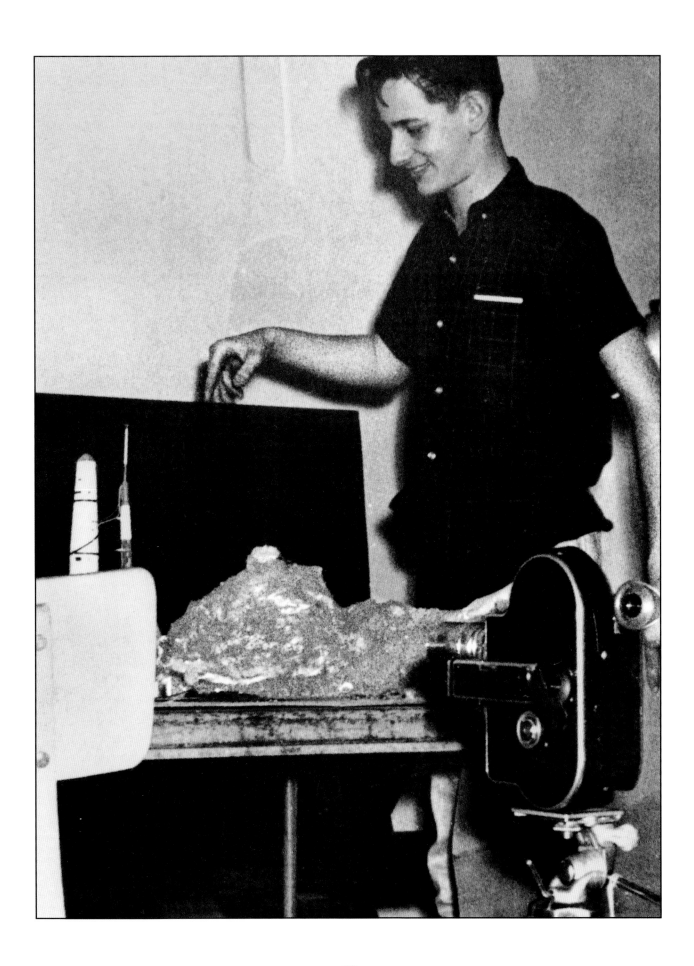

the films that Steven would later make are the direct results of his relationship with his parents and his sisters. He also loved scaring people and delighted in hearing his sisters scream, knowing he was the cause of it.

"I loved terrifying them to the point of cardiac arrest," Steven admitted. "I remember a movie on television with a Martian who kept a severed head in a fishbowl. It scared them so much they couldn't watch it. So I locked them in a closet with a fishbowl. I can still hear the terror breaking in their voices."

THE FIRST CAMERA

While his sisters provided targets for Steven's playful tricks and mean-spirited harassment, it was his father who gave him the freedom to take his mischievous quest for amusement into new territory. When eight-year-old Steven took the family movie camera from his father during a family vacation, Arnold saw the first signs of his son's incredible talent for composing images in the frame, for capturing just the right moment, in just the right light or shadow.

Over the next several years, Arnold bought all the 8mm film and camera, sound, and editing equipment that his son needed to turn this childhood hobby of home movie-making

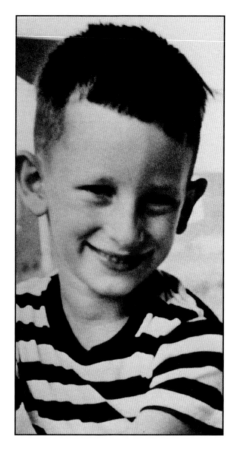

As a child, Steven was sometimes shy, always mischievous, and seemed to have been born with a love of movies and a desire to find new ways of using a camera.

into a career quest—a quest borne out of two very specific events from Steven's early childhood.

When Steven was five years old, his father took him to see Cecil B. DeMille's *The Greatest Show on Earth*. Steven cried because the circus in the movie, which looked so convincing, wasn't real. After that experience, however, Steven became fascinated with the idea that something—anything—could be made to appear real on film. This respect for cinema became the core of Steven's personality.

Later, when Steven was in the fourth grade, the family moved to Arizona. He tells this story: "One night my dad woke me up in the middle of the night and rushed me into our car in my night clothes. I didn't know what was happening. It was frightening. My mom wasn't with me. So I thought, *What's happening here? . . .* we drove for about a half an hour. We finally pulled over to the side of the road, and there were a couple hundred people, lying on their backs in the middle of the night, looking up at the sky. [My dad] pointed to the sky, and there was a magnificent meteor shower. All these incredible points of light were crisscrossing the sky."

A YOUNG MOVIEMAKER

Making movies was Steven's way of cop-
ing with the loneliness he felt as a child.
His family moved several times, and
forming relationships wasn't easy for
Steven. Just as he would make new
friends, the family would move.

His Jewish heritage made things
even more difficult, because few Jewish
people lived in the neighborhoods where
the Spielbergs lived. In high school,
Steven suffered prejudice and
wasn't accepted by many of
his classmates.

Steven escaped deeper
into the imaginary world of the
movies. "Once I could make films,"
Steven said, "I found I could create
a great day or a great week just by
creating a story. . . . I found I could
do anything or live anywhere via
my imagination, through film."

Performing in his
movies were Steven's sisters,
the neighborhood kids,
and even his mother on
occasion. He experi-
mented with the camera,
but his first real attempt to
make a story-film was at
age 12, as a member of
the Boy Scout's Troop 294.
Despite the limitations of his
equipment, the quality of Steven's
films continued to improve. By age 16,

his films' realism earned him not only a local reputation, but statewide contest honors at the Canyon Films Junior Film Festival.

Then life changed for Steven. When he graduated from high school in 1965, Steven's father left the family and moved to Los Angeles. His parents filed for divorce the following year. Steven was devastated by the breakup of his family and buried himself in his work, pursuing with a vengeance his goal of becoming a professional filmmaker. He applied to the prestigious film schools at the University of California, Los Angeles, and the University of Southern California, but his applications were rejected by both schools. He instead attended California State College at Long Beach and, as he recalled, "did almost nothing except watch movies and make movies."

He studied the work of other student filmmakers, John Milius, Francis Ford Coppola, and a rising young talent named George Lucas—all of whom were enrolled in the schools that had rejected Steven. Recalling one of Lucas's student films, a science fiction thriller called *THX:1138:4EB*, Steven admitted to feeling "jealous to the marrow of [his] bones."

As a student, Steven absorbed as much knowledge about film as he could; now he's taken on the role of educator to teach the value of film as a tool against racism, discrimination, and anti-Semitism.

THE BIG BREAK

Steven's films were being viewed as well—by producers at Universal Studios. Steven shopped his wares around to anyone who would watch. He made a film called *Amblin'*, which impressed the right people, and in the fall of 1968 Steven was offered a seven-year contract with Universal. Given this fantastic opportunity, Steven dropped out of college and turned his full attention to Hollywood.

His first project was one story in a three-part TV movie called *Night Gallery*. His challenge was directing film legend Joan Crawford. "I was so frightened," Steven recalled. "I was walking on eggs."

In 1971 Steven was offered the chance to direct a made-for-television movie called *Duel*. It is the story of a man pursued by a truck driver while traveling a lonely canyon highway. It was Steven's chance to do what he had always done best—terrify people. In his hands, *Duel* became a reflection of the human fear of being chased by a merciless monster—a theme that has since become a hallmark of many Spielberg films, including his first big hit, *Jaws*.

In telling the story of a man-eating shark that terrorizes a quiet vacation community, Steven played on his audience's fear of the unknown, the unseen. For the first half of the movie, only the shark's dorsal fin is shown, but it's more than enough to turn a viewer's blood to ice. Steven's reliance on the audience's imagination would be the cornerstone of his developing film style. Today, *Jaws* is considered a masterpiece, and, released in 1975, it was the first film in history to make more than 100 million dollars at the box office. Its director wasn't yet 30 years old.

LIFE IN HOLLYWOOD

With that kind of success, Steven could now write his own ticket in Hollywood—and he did. Because Steven had always gotten what he felt he needed to do his best work (once Leah let her young son spew cherry pie filling all over their kitchen cabinets and walls to simulate the results of an explosion), he was fearless in making demands from his studio, Columbia Pictures. The cost of making his next film, *Close Encounters*, quickly rose from the budgeted $2.7 to $5.5 million dollars, yet Steven kept insisting he needed more money. When the final cost came in at $19 million dollars, Steven had everyone, including his nearly bankrupt studio, terrified of failure.

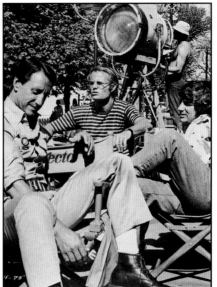

Like his idol, director David Lean (opposite below), who made Bridge on the River Kwai, *Steven is both playful and serious on the set, involving himself in everything from props and special effects to soundtracks and even marketing.*

Once again, Steven proved successful. *Close Encounters* grossed 270 million dollars and sent Columbia's profits soaring. Steven was nominated for an Academy Award as Best Director that year, but he didn't win—due in large part, many critics believe, because veteran filmmakers were resentful of this young director who seemed to have found instant success. No one realized that Steven had now been making films for twenty years.

What Steven himself didn't realize until that time was that he had been spending *all* his time making films. He still didn't have any close friends, he didn't spend a lot of time with his family, and he rarely dated. Forming relationships had never been easy for Steven. He was afraid of getting too close to people because he was afraid of losing them, just as he had lost so many childhood friends when his family moved from place to place.

When he met actress Amy Irving in 1977, he finally let himself get close, and soon the two fell in love. Steven had a complicated personality, though. He was passionate about his work, and often found it difficult to balance all the elements in his life. His mother and sisters had come to understand this, but Amy couldn't. She and Steven stayed together only four years. Though they reunited three years later, married, and had a son they named Max, the marriage didn't last.

Amidst the growing demands of his work—which often took him away from home for several months at a time—Steven struggled to maintain his personal relationships; he was devastated by the breakup of his marriage to Amy Irving.

One friend who did understand Steven's passion for film was fellow filmmaker George Lucas. Shortly after the first break-up with Amy, Steven vacationed with George in Hawaii to talk about doing a project together. As they talked, the two discovered that they both loved the old Saturday matinee serials, and George presented Steven with an idea for a movie about an adventuring archeologist named Indiana Jones.

George would write and Steven would direct. What followed would become legendary. "Steven was drawn to it as an opportunity to reinvent the films that he had seen when he was growing up," said the star of *Raiders of the Lost Ark*, Harrison Ford.

There were no man-eating sharks in *Raiders*, but there was something even more appealing to Steven: Nazis and the wrath of God. In pain over his failed relationship with Amy, Steven's inherent need to terrify people in retaliation surfaced. Though intending—and succeeding—to make the film fun and exciting, he pushed himself to create graphic images of terror, including skeletons popping from dark corners and Nazi faces melting from their bones.

Steven received his second Oscar nomination for Best Director, but again he was passed over, and it hurt. He was Hollywood's *wunderkind.* His brilliance as a filmmaker was never questioned by the critics. His films, though, seemed less respectable than those of award-winning filmmakers, whose work appeared to come from places deep and serious. With that in mind, Steven decided it was time to open himself up to his audience. His goal in filmmaking had always been the presentation of reality, but now it was time to add something more: truth.

ALL THE RIGHT CHOICES

"With *E.T.* I'd always wanted to tell the story of a . . . lonely boy in a relationship with siblings, and I also wanted to tell the story about the divorce of my parents," Steven revealed. Like the many films that would follow, as Steven developed the story he was about to shoot, he found himself rediscovering his own childhood. Drawing from those memories—his yearning for friendship and the painful departure of his father—Steven's extra-terrestrial creation would in fact be a mirror image of himself. "The friendship that E.T. and Elliot find and hold on to—clinging to each other desperately—is sort of what I went through. I wished I had had a best friend."

Steven has always loved working with children, and the film E.T. offered him a challenging opportunity to tell a story from the unique point of view of children; he even endowed the character of E.T. with childlike qualities.

In actuality, Steven has lots of friends, people who respect and admire him, people who trust him. Two of those people are Frank Marshall and Kathleen Kennedy, producers who teamed up with Steven in 1984 to form Amblin Entertainment. They produce films and television shows, including the medical drama *ER*, which was created by Michael Crichton, the author of *Jurassic Park*. Like Steven's films, *ER* has been hailed by critics who see Steven's insistence on reality and truth as a key element in the success of his work.

Steven's other production company was formed in 1994 when he joined producers David Geffen and Jeffrey Katzenberg in forming DreamWorks SKG, a film company that would be dedicated to creating intelligent and innovative movies. Their projects include *Amistad, Mousehunt,* and the animated features, *Antz* and *Prince of Egypt.*

Steven's best partnership, however, is with wife Kate Capshaw. With his son Max; Kate's daughter, Jessica, from a previous marriage; three children of their own; and two adopted children, Steven finally has the stable family that he had longed for as a youngster.

Steven has made career choices that have allowed him to be close to his family. He works fewer days, and he spends as much time at home with his children as he can. He even turned down an offer to run Walt Disney Pictures in favor of remaining in control of his own project schedule. "I realized that [by working nonstop] I could be a [Walt] Disney, but that I would be a terrible father, or I could forget Disney and be a great father."

Part of being a good parent, Steven believes, is being respectful of one's cultural heritage. Growing up in a Jewish family living in non-Jewish neighborhoods was difficult for Steven, and he rejected his heritage for a long time. After the birth of Max, he started moving back toward his faith. When he married Kate and began adding to his family, Steven not only faced his Jewish background, he embraced it. Likewise, as a filmmaker, Steven felt it necessary to face an important part of Jewish history: the Holocaust.

A PERSONAL JOURNEY

Steven wanted to make a film version of Thomas Keneally's book *Schindler's List* the moment he finished reading it, but it was a number of years before he felt emotionally "ready" to make the film. The studio pushed him to make *Jurassic Park* first, knowing that the making of *Schindler's List* might change Steven forever. They were right.

Steven relied on Kate for support during the making of Schindler's List, which led him to gather with survivors of the Holocaust at Oskar Schindler's memorial (center). For the film's title role, Steven chose Liam Neeson, a tall, commanding actor from Europe.

When the time came to make *Schindler's List*, he arranged with the studio to take no director's salary for the work, feeling he would be profiting from the suffering of others. Also, he donated his contract percentage of the profits to Jewish organizations and historical projects such as the United States Holocaust Memorial Museum in Washington, D.C. He also used some of the money to establish the Survivors of the Shoah Visual History Foundation, which records the oral histories of Holocaust survivors, and the Righteous Persons Foundation, which provides grants for Jewish groups.

Schindler's List is a brutally honest telling of the horrors of the Holocaust. Steven found that filming it at the very sites where millions of Jews were once tortured and killed was the most emotionally draining experience of his life. He took his wife and children with him to Kraków, Poland, for emotional support. "My kids saw me cry for the first time," Steven said. "I would come home and weep, not because I was feeling sorry for anybody—I would weep because it was *so bloody painful.*"

Shot in stark black-and-white, the three-hour film received 12 Academy Award nominations—including one for Steven as Best Director. Cheers erupted the night of March 21, 1994, when the envelope was opened and the award for Best Director was announced: Steven Spielberg. In his acceptance speech, Steven thanked his wife, Kate, who had converted to the Jewish faith, "for rescuing [him] ninety-two days in a row, in Kraków, Poland, when things got just too unbearable."

Schindler's List won six more awards, including Best Picture. With this achievement, Steven had finally won Hollywood's respect—he was finally considered a *serious* filmmaker. The experience of *Schindler's List* was a turning point in Steven's life. "I feel I have a responsibility, and I want to go back and forth from entertainment to socially conscious movies."

True to this word, he made *The Lost World*, the sequel to *Jurassic Park*, and then went on to create arguably the most realistic story of war that has ever been put to film. Having always been fascinated by the history of World War II, Steven envisioned his three-hour drama, *Saving Private Ryan*, as a singular image of the personal horrors of war. In the lead was Steven's good friend Tom Hanks, who worked hard and never complained about the grueling task of

Technology was a tool that Steven used to create the sense of reality and wonder in Jurassic Park *and* The Lost World, *but making his actors go through a type of harsh boot camp before filming is what helped make* Saving Private Ryan *so truthful and real.*

bringing the D-Day invasion to life. Directing thousands of extras over weeks of shooting the movie, Steven choreographed every shot, every scene to perfection. With explosions and gunfire everywhere, amazingly, no one was hurt during filming.

Tom Hanks admits that the film is "gruesome, because war is." Steven advises that, although he believes this is an important film, "nobody fourteen years old or under should see it." While the commercial success of *Private Ryan* didn't reach "Jurassic" numbers (*Jurassic Park* made $900 million), a string of Academy Award nominations—and another win for Best Director—clearly attest to the film's craftsmanship.

Recognized as one of the greatest filmmakers of all time, Steven finds it ironic that his style of filmmaking hasn't changed at all from the days when he was making volcanoes erupt in his parents' garage—he's always made his movies real, he's always told a universal truth. Steven Spielberg has been doing it right all along.

V O I C E S

On the early years:

"I knew that here was a very bright new director. Steven . . . has this extraordinary size of vision, a sweep that illuminates his films. But then, Steven is the way the movies used to be."

David Lean, director and
Steven's idol

"The director of that movie is the greatest young talent to come along in years."

Veteran filmmaker Billy Wilder
in 1974, after a preview of The
Sugarland Express

"Every film is an experience. I'll be learning when I'm sixty years old. I've learned more out on my own than I'll ever learn inside a studio."

Steven Spielberg, late 1960s

"[In making *Jaws*,] "Steven found himself facing an opportunity to have himself tested in a way that few people ever have. It's as if he had prepared himself for that moment from the time he was ten years old. He knew that he could be everything that he wanted to be after that summer."

    Richard Dreyfuss, Jaws

ON HIS FILMS:

"Watching this vibrantly comic, boundlessly touching fantasy, you feel that Spielberg has, for the first time, put his breathtaking technical skills at the service of his deepest feelings."

    Rolling Stones' *Michael Sragow on* E.T.: The Extra-Terrestrial

"I believe that the success of *Close Encounters of the Third Kind* comes from Steven's very special gift for giving plausibility to the extraordinary."

    François Truffaut, actor/director

Steven draws from memories of his own childhood to successfully draw honest emotions out of his child actors; from pain and sadness to excitement and joy, Steven knows just how to lead an actor to the heart of a scene.

"This is not simply a good movie. It is one of the rare movies that brush away our cautions and win our hearts."

> *Film critic Roger Ebert on*
> E.T.: The Extra-Terrestrial

"*Poltergeist* is what I fear and *E.T.* is what I love. One is about suburban evil, and the other is about suburban good . . . *Poltergeist* is the darker side of my nature—it's me when I was scaring my younger sisters half to death when we were growing up."

> *Steven Spielberg*

"If *Schindler's List* was Spielberg's rite of passage from starry-eyed man-child to a more serious, morality-driven filmmaker, then *Saving Private Ryan* showed him making good on that promise."

> *Chris Nashawaty,*
> Entertainment Weekly

ON WORKING WITH STEVEN:

"When you work with him he's Thomas Edison inventing the lightbulb. He's a genius."

> *Tom Hanks,*
> Saving Private Ryan

As a fearless yet sensitive film artist, Steven is highly regarded as the best in his field today, both by critics such as Roger Ebert (top) and by actors as diverse in background as Anthony Hopkins (center) and Tom Hanks (bottom).

"He moved very, very fast. And it was fantastic."

Liam Neeson,
Schindler's List

"[Steven wanted to] complicate his personality as much as possible—to give him some real emotions."

Harrison Ford, on the creation of the Indiana Jones character

"Steven Spielberg really changed my life 'cause he was the model to say 'this is how you do it.' He goes for the truth every time."

Oprah Winfrey,
The Color Purple

O N   C H O O S I N G   H I S S U B J E C T S :

"Before I had Max, I made films about kids; now that I have one, I'll probably start making films about adults."

Steven Spielberg, 1985,
after the birth of his son

"[When we talked about doing *Schindler's List*] we knew that where we were going would be so painful, so sad—it was going to make us so angry."

Kate Capshaw

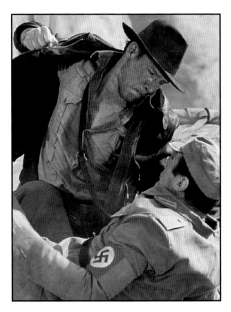

One underlying theme in all of Steven's films involves human rights, be it an ant's right to choose his career path, the threat against human rights by groups such as the Nazi Party, or the right to freedom from slavery.

"Lost boys and lost children: that's the subject that most powerfully moves him."

> *Richard Schikel, film critic*

ON STEVEN SPIELBERG:

"I think the thing that would be the most surprising thing about Steven to the world would be how easily he gets his feelings hurt."

> *Kate Capshaw*

"When he was growing up, I didn't know he was a genius. Frankly, I didn't know what he was."

> *Leah Adler, Steven*
> *Spielberg's mother*

"A very large part of who I am as a human being and who I've become is due to him."

> *Drew Barrymore,*
> *E.T.: The Extra-Terrestrial*

"Steven is just this guy who period-ically rewrites the book on how films are made."

> *Tom Hanks*

Steven has always made people his first concern, as when he founded the Star-bright Foundation for children with serious illnesses—something that makes Steven's mother especially proud of her son.

OVATIONS